A CENTURY *of* EXETER

Central High Street taken from the Guildhall, *c.* 1930.

A CENTURY *of* EXETER

PETER THOMAS

SUTTON PUBLISHING

First published in the United Kingdom in 1999 by
Sutton Publishing Limited · Phoenix Mill
Thrupp · Stroud · Gloucestershire · GL5 2BU

British Library Cataloguing in Publication Data
A catalogue record for this book is available from the British Library.

ISBN 0-7509-2427-6

Front endpaper: Aerial view of Exeter, *c.* 1930.
Back endpaper: The north Exe Bridge, 1999. In the post-war years Exeter's riverside areas have been subject to massive changes. The entrance into Exeter from the west was one of its great charms. Today bridges are made in concrete and are purely functional. The riverbanks, now concreted to assist with flood control, give an opportunity to walk the banks of the controlled river system.
Half title page: The Globe Hotel, Cathedral Yard, *c.* 1930. The hotel was lost in the Exeter Blitz, May 1942.
Title page: Northernhay Place with the Plaza cinema, *c.* 1930.

Typeset in 11/14pt Photina.
Typesetting and origination by
Sutton Publishing Limited.
Printed in Great Britain by
The Bath Press, Bath.

The Mayor drives the last electric tram, 1931.

Contents

Family group in lane off Stepcote Hill, *c.* 1910.

Britain: A Century of Change

Children gathered around an early wireless set in the 1920s. The speed and forms of communication were to change dramatically as the century advanced. (*Barnaby's Picture Library*)

The delirious rejoicing at the news of the Relief of Mafeking, during the Boer War in May 1900, is a colourful historical moment. But, in retrospect, the introduction that year of the first motor bus was rather more important, signalling another major adjustment to town life. In the previous 60 years railway stations, post-and-telegraph offices, police and fire stations, gas works and gasometers, new livestock markets and covered markets, schools, churches, football grounds, hospitals and asylums, water pumping stations and sewerage plants had totally altered the urban scene, as the country's population tripled and over 70 per cent were born in or moved to the towns.

When Queen Victoria died in 1901, she was measured for her coffin by her grandson Kaiser Wilhelm, the London prostitutes put on black mourning and the blinds came down in the villas and terraces spreading out from the old town centres. These centres were reachable by train and tram, by the new bicycles and still newer motor cars, connected by the new telephone, and lit by gas or even electricity. The shops may have been full of British-made cotton and woollen clothing but the grocers and butchers were selling cheap Danish bacon, Argentinian beef, Australasian mutton, tinned or dried fish and fruit from Canada, California and South Africa. Most of these goods were carried in British-built-and-crewed ships, burning Welsh steam coal.

Women working as porters on the Great Western Railway, Paddington, *c.* 1917. (*W.L. Kenning/ Adrian Vaughan Collection*)

As the first decade moved on, the Open Spaces Act meant more parks, bowling greens and cricket pitches. The first state pensions came in, together with higher taxation and death duties. These were raised mostly to pay for the new Dreadnought battleships needed to maintain naval superiority over Germany, and deter them from war. But the deterrent did not work. The First World War transformed the place of women, as they took over many men's jobs. Its other legacies were the war memorials which joined the statues of Victorian worthies in main squares round the land. After 1918 death duties bit even harder and a quarter of England changed hands in a few years.

The multiple shop – the chain store – appeared in the high street: Sainsburys, Maypole, Lipton's, Home & Colonial, the Fifty Shilling Tailor, Burton, Boots, W.H. Smith. The shopper was spoilt for choice, attracted by the brash fascias and advertising hoardings for national brands like Bovril, Pears Soap, and Ovaltine. Many new buildings began to be seen, such as garages, motor showrooms, picture palaces (cinemas), 'palais de dance', and the bow-windowed, pebble-dashed, tile-hung, half-timbered houses that were built as ribbon-development along the roads and new bypasses or on the new estates nudging the green belts.

During the 1920s cars became more reliable and sophisticated as well as commonplace, with developments like the electric self-starter making them easier for women to drive. Who wanted to turn a crank handle in the new short skirt? This was, indeed, the electric age as much as the motor era. Trolley buses, electric trams and trains extended mass transport and electric light replaced gas in the street and the home, which itself was groomed by the vacuum cleaner.

Father and child cycling past Buckingham Palace on VE Day, 8 May 1945. (*Hulton Getty Picture Collection*)

A major jolt to the march onward and upward was administered by the Great Depression of the early 1930s. The older British industries – textiles, shipbuilding, iron, steel, coal – were already under pressure from foreign competition when this worldwide slump arrived, cutting exports by half in two years and producing 3 million unemployed (and still rising) by 1932. Luckily there were new diversions to alleviate the misery. The 'talkies' arrived in the cinemas; more and more radios and gramophones were to be found in people's homes; there were new women's magazines, with fashion, cookery tips and problem pages; football pools; the flying feats of women pilots like Amy Johnson; the Loch Ness Monster; cheap chocolate and the drama of Edward VIII's abdication.

Things were looking up again by 1936 and unemployment was down to 2 million. New light industry was booming in the Home Counties as factories struggled to keep up with the demand for radios, radiograms, cars and electronic goods including the first television sets. The threat from Hitler's Germany meant rearmament, particularly of the airforce, which stimulated aircraft and aero engine firms. If you were lucky and lived in the south, there was good money to be earned. A semi-detached house cost £450, a Morris Cowley £150. People may have smoked like chimneys but life expectancy, since 1918, was up by 15 years while the birth rate had almost halved. The fifty-four hour week was down to forty-eight hours and there were 9 million radio licences by 1939.

In some ways it is the little memories that seem to linger longest from the Second World War: the kerbs painted white to show up in the blackout, the rattle of ack-ack shrapnel on roof tiles, sparrows killed by bomb blast, painting your legs brown and then adding a black seam

A family gathered around their television set in the 1950s. (*Hulton Getty Picture Collection*)

down the back to simulate stockings. The biggest damage, apart from London, was in the south-west (Plymouth, Bristol) and the Midlands (Coventry, Birmingham). Postwar reconstruction was rooted in the Beveridge Report which set out the expectations for the Welfare State. This, together with the nationalisation of the Bank of England, coal, gas, electricity and the railways, formed the programme of the Labour government in 1945. At this time the USA was calling in its debts and Britain was beggared by the war, yet still administering its Empire.

Times were hard in the late 1940s, with rationing even more stringent than during the war. Yet this was, as has been said, 'an innocent and well-behaved era'. The first let-up came in 1951 with the Festival of Britain and then there was another fillip in 1953 from the Coronation, which incidentally gave a huge boost to the spread of TV. By 1954 leisure motoring had been resumed but the Comet – Britain's best hope for taking on the American aviation industry – suffered a series of mysterious crashes. The Suez debacle of 1956 was followed by an acceleration in the withdrawal from Empire, which had begun in 1947 with the Independence of India. Consumerism was truly born with the advent of commercial TV and most homes soon boasted washing machines, fridges, electric irons and fires.

The *Lady Chatterley* obscenity trial in 1960 was something of a straw in the wind for what was to follow in that decade. A collective loss of inhibition seemed to sweep the land, as stately home owners opened up, the Beatles and the Rolling Stones transformed popular music, and retailing, cinema and the theatre were revolutionised. Designers, hairdressers, photographers and models moved into places vacated by an Establishment put to flight by the new breed of satirists spawned by *Beyond the Fringe* and *Private Eye*.

In the 1970s Britain seems to have suffered a prolonged hangover after the excesses of the previous decade. Ulster, inflation and union troubles were not made up for by entry into the EEC, North Sea Oil, Women's Lib or, indeed, Punk Rock. Mrs Thatcher applied the corrective in the 1980s, as the country moved more and more from its old manufacturing base over to providing services, consulting, advertising, and expertise in the 'invisible' market of high finance or in IT. Britain entertained the world with *Cats*, *Phantom of the Opera*, *Four Weddings and a Funeral*, *The Full Monty*, *Mr Bean* and the *Teletubbies*.

Carnaby Street in the 1960s. (*Barnaby's Picture Library*)

The post-1945 townscape has seen changes to match those in the worlds of work, entertainment and politics. In 1956 the Clean Air Act served notice on smogs and pea-souper fogs, smuts and blackened buildings, forcing people to stop burning coal and go over to smokeless sources of heat and energy. In the same decade some of the best urban building took place in the 'new towns' like Basildon, Crawley, Stevenage and Harlow. Elsewhere open warfare was declared on slums and what was labelled inadequate, cramped, back-to-back, two-up, two-down, housing. The new 'machine for living in' was a flat in a high-rise block. The architects and planners who promoted these were in league with the traffic engineers, determined to keep the motor car moving whatever the price in multi-storey car parks, meters, traffic wardens and ring roads.

The Millennium Dome at Greenwich, 1999. (*Michael Durnan/Barnaby's Picture Library*)

The old pollutant, coal smoke, was replaced by petrol and diesel exhaust, and traffic noise. Even in the back garden it was hard to find peace as motor mowers, then leaf blowers and strimmers made themselves heard, and the neighbours let you share their choice of music from their powerful new amplifiers, whether you wanted to or not. Fast food was no longer only a pork pie in a pub or fish-and-chips. There were Indian curry houses, Chinese take-aways and American-style hamburgers, while the drinker could get away from beer in a wine bar. Under the impact of television the big Gaumonts and Odeons closed or were rebuilt as multi-screen cinemas, while the palais de dance gave way to discos and clubs.

From the late 1960s the introduction of listed buildings and conservation areas, together with the growth of preservation societies, put a brake on 'comprehensive redevelopment'. Now the new risk at the end of the 1990s is that town centres may die, as shoppers are attracted to the edge-of-town supermarkets surrounded by parking space, where much more than food and groceries can be bought. The ease of the one-stop shop represents the latest challenge to the good health of our towns. But with care, ingenuity and a determination to keep control of our environment, this challenge can be met.

Exeter: An Introduction

Exeter, the capital of Devon, occupies an unsurpassed location overlooking the River Exe. Situated in lush countryside, the city is recognised as having a particularly high quality of life. Those who live here know the advantages, and each year thousands of visitors use Exeter as their gateway to the west. Most people are genuinely captured by the city's charms.

Traditionally Exeter has continued its way of life within its stone walls changing only slowly over the centuries; however, this was to alter in the eighteenth and nineteenth centuries. Exeter was to change in some respects beyond recognition.

In this book we shall be looking at some aspects of what has happened to Exeter over the last 100 years. It has been a time of great physical change. From the very turn of the century Exeter was to grasp new opportunities and ideas. As it did so, many Exeter residents began to see enormous changes to the environment in which they had grown up. Our century is well divided from 1900 to approximately 1939; the

Re-enactment of roman Exeter in Bury Meadow, Exeter Pageant, 1902.

Second World War from 1939; the postwar development to around 1970; and the last thirty years. Today further changes are under way as the city continues to expand rapidly.

Exeter has always been a busy market town and this continues today, generating income for the city, but now well out of the city centre. In Victorian times the streets were cleared and purpose-built markets were created. Cattle, however, were sold at the Cattle Market beside Exe Bridge in Bonhay Road. A move was then made to Marsh Barton, and in recent years Matford.

Exeter can never lay claim to being an industrial city, but there were some heavy industries. Now long gone, they played an important role in the economy of the city.

In the first half of this century the city still retained numerous old buildings and an atmosphere of times gone by. At the turn of the century a new bridge was to be constructed over the River Exe, and with it the introduction of an electric tram system. Extending from the bridge, buildings were removed and new riverside walkways created. The era of public transport had begun.

Social life was to broaden with the opening of Dellers Café in the Cathedral Close in 1906, followed by the opening of their prestigious premises on the corner of High Street and Bedford Street in 1916.

Eastmans of Exeter, late 1930s. Although the exact location of these premises is unknown they show very well a typical shop interior of the period.

In 1907 restoration of one of the city's most prestigious buildings, 226 High Street, took place. In 1911 Rougemont House and grounds were purchased by the City Council, and the grounds were opened to the public in 1912. St Nicholas Priory was also purchased at this time by the Council and opened as a museum.

In the 1920s many people left the Goldsmith Street area, and there was a period of demolition. A major loss was 229 High Street (now Topshop), whose Jacobean interior was ripped out by the Saxone Shoe Company and exported to America. It can now be seen in the Kansas City Museum. The building as it stands today is a sad contrivance of architectural remains saved from other buildings. St Stephen's Church in High Street was also threatened with demolition. In High Street almost opposite St Petrock's Church was the double-fronted shop of Garton and King, ironmongers. Their premises extended back to Waterbeer Street, and their foundry was on the other side of the street. They left the site in 1932.

Street traders at Christmas in Milk Street, off Fore Street, *c.* 1932. The side of the lower market can be seen in the rear – now the site of St George's Market.

Much of Exeter's social life revolved around the London Inn Square, whose focal point up to 1936 was the New London Hotel. The old coaching inn was removed to allow the building of the Savoy Cinema. Other losses in this period were St Paul's Church in Paul Street and St John's Church in Fore Street.

In the 1930s a slum clearance scheme moved citizens out to the suburbs and demolished dwellings. This policy created the Burnthouse Lane Housing Estate. Despite this happening sixty years ago people still talk of their times in the West Quarter. Our most famous street, Stepcote Hill, was to lose over 50 per cent of its buildings. The modern replacements failed to complement those remaining. Two sixteenth-century buildings at the bottom of the Hill were saved after a public outcry. They now form part of one of Exeter's loveliest settings. The city, however, fails to recognise fully the potential of this area.

Unfortunately Exeter suffered badly with bombing from 1939 to 1942. It sustained seventeen air raids and a third of the city centre was

A view of the Cathedral yard from the north tower of Exeter Cathedral showing the Globe Hotel, *c.* 1935.

destroyed. All remaining standing buildings were demolished by the City Council. The clearance of the central area of Exeter opened up new opportunities to redevelop the city, and this was undertaken from the 1950s to approximately 1970. The rebuilding has been much criticised, as it is said a monolithic style inappropriate for the city was adopted. The individuality of varying architectural styles was lost. For example, the building of C & A on the corner of High Street and Queen Street was to prove highly controversial, with the intrusion of an ugly structure right in the middle of High Street. The previous elegant façade could have been recreated on such a sensitive site. It stands for all to see and is one of Exeter's greatest errors.

In the 1970s further development took place – the Golden Heart Project. It involved the demolition of the whole area from Queen Street to North Street, and from Paul Street to High Street. Goldsmith Street, one of Exeter's oldest thoroughfares, was utterly destroyed. The Higher Market was also affected by the scheme, with the loss of its rear steps.

Modelling the latest clothes for a fashion show in Colsons, High Street, 1948.

Featureless shops were built into its lofty interior, and nearly all of its character was lost. Paul Street was swept away and the ugliest service road in Exeter created. The scheme also devastated a fine building in North Street, dating from the fifteenth century but with seventeenth-century additions. This was 38 North Street, which was totally demolished. Today North Street is a sad introduction to Exeter.

In latter years great attempts have been made to soften some of these early developments with the planting of thousands of trees, the creation of gardens, the addition of street furniture and so on.

The compactness of the city centre makes shopping easy and it boasts a huge number of shops. The Cathedral Close continues to ooze old-world charm, and is one of the city's most pleasant environments.

Now, with the Millennium imminent, *A Century of Exeter* with its wide range of images, reflects the most important period in Exeter's past. It will also help us to focus on the future of one of England's most ancient cities.

J. Hinton Lake, at No. 41 High Street, was a famous chemist, *c.* 1915. This site is currently occupied by Laura Ashley.

1900–1920

Shipping at the Quay, *c.* 1900. It is difficult today to imagine vessels of this nature moored at Exeter's Quay. It has been suggested that in times gone by ships could have been seen moored three deep running along the Quay, with packages and crates covering the quayside. Huge quantities of coal were imported into Exeter and a number of coalyards were found in the area. Two merchandising companies ran six vessels per week to and fro to London. Beside the two vessels shown can be seen Rose Cottage, which was to become the home of the ferryman after demolition of the original ferryman's cottage on the Quay in the 1830s.

Two horse-drawn trams are shown at a crossing point in Sidwell Street outside the White Lion Hotel, *c.* 1900. Only four routes were used by the horse trams. The first vehicle clearly indicates East Gate, Bath Road & Mount Pleasant; the second Eastgate, Paris Street and Heavitree. The horse tramways operated after 14 July 1881 until the advent of the electric trams. The cost of a ride was 1*d*. Twelve people could sit inside and twelve on the top. The route to St David's cost 3*d* – and it must have been an interesting sight to see the horses pulling a full load up St Davids Hill!

In 1901 a decision was made to refurbish and re-hang the Cathedral bells. To modernise the system it was necessary to construct a complete new iron cage, which would make ringing a far easier task. It was found that some of the bells had to be recast, including the tenor and fifth bells. This was done by a firm in Loughborough. Part of the costs were paid by the public and part by the Dean and Chapter. A re-dedication service took place on 24 June 1902, and the bells were re-hung in time for the coronation of Edward VII in 1902. This photograph shows the arrival of a bell by horse and cart outside the west front of the Cathedral. Its tone is checked by a young boy who is tapping it.

Above: In February 1902 a public meeting took place in the Guildhall to discuss how the city could celebrate the coronation of Edward VII. From that meeting sprang the idea of a major historical pageant: the idea was put forward by Mr Willey, one of Exeter's most prominent businessmen. The pageant, in which over 600 people took part, represented the whole of English history. A huge procession took place with horse-drawn tableaux. Taken from a lantern slide, this photograph shows a tableau entering Bedford Circus: it depicts the Wars of the Roses, with Henry VI receiving the keys of the South Gate surrounded by nobles.

Exeter Pageant, 1902.

The three-arched stone Exe Bridge, *c.* 1902. At the turn of the century the entry into the city from the west was far more elegant than it is today. Spanning the River Exe was a three-arched stone bridge completed in 1778. The views up river at this time were far more rural. Trees lined the river banks. Buildings met the bridge on both sides of the river giving a far more friendly feel to entering Exeter. The bridge shown replaced the early medieval bridge. Although mostly demolished the medieval bridge was partially retained and still formed Edmund Street, giving access to West Street. A new road was built to meet the stone bridge, New Bridge Street, which involved breaching the city wall. Today the 1905 bridge and nearly all the buildings shown no longer exist.

The demolition of the old stone bridge, 1904. A decision to introduce a new electric tram system and a new bridge was to lead to the building of a wooden pontoon bridge. It was constructed to allow continued public access over the river. Its high sides are seen on the right. Here the stone bridge is being dismantled. The road surface is now exposed and the top of the central arch is showing. The elegant balustrades each side have been taken away and were sold off. Some can still be seen around an entrance in Exwick.

Workers at Exe Bridge, 1905. The local company of Woodmans was involved in the construction of the new bridge. Here the workers stop to be recorded as part of the city's most prestigious project.

The construction of the new Exe Bridge, 1904–5. The new bridge is here nearing completion. It was to be opened in March 1905. The cost of construction was £25,000 and it was designed by Sir John Wolfe Barry and Mr C.A. Brereton. The span was said to be the flattest in the country and was based on a three-hinged arch to allow for expansion and contraction. Massive granite bed-stones took the thrust of the arches. Red shale from Mortonhampstead was used as its foundation. The vessel moored at the bridge appears to have a cargo of huge stone blocks.

The Opening of Exe Bridge, 1905. On 29 March 1905 the new steel Exe Bridge was opened by the Mayor, Councillor C. Perry. There was a huge celebration, and a military escort. A rope was suspended from the traction poles on each side of the bridge and duly cut by the Mayor to open the bridge. Part of the rope still exists today, complete with label indicating its use. Such was the interest in the ceremony that people climbed on to their roofs to view the scene. The wooden pontoon bridge, which had not yet been removed, is on the left.

Exe Bridge Memorial Card, 1905.

The completed Exe Bridge, 1905. Exeter's new bridge, built at a cost of £25,000, and the electric tram system, started a new era for the city. The new bridge was to give better pedestrian access with an 8 ft wide path, and the road width had been extended to 36 ft. The movement of a tram can be seen on the left. On the St Thomas side Randal's the seed merchants advertise 'The British Lion Pea is unequalled for crop and exhibition'. On the edge of the bridge, right, Hucklebridge & Sons, Engineers, declare their interest in 'Sanitary and Hydraulic work, Steam and Hot water heating, Electric and Gas lighting'. Overlooking the river is the photographic studio of the Crown Photo Co. Above their windows can be seen the roof of the daylight studio.

The laying of tram lines, 1903. Great curiosity is expressed by Exeter citizens as the new tram lines are laid in High Street and Queen Street. In 1903 a bill was passed for the creation of 6 miles of track across the city along nine defined routes. A Committee and Chairman were to be elected to oversee the introduction of the new system and shopkeepers rapidly benefited from increased trade. At this time the shop shown right on the corner of Queen Street was occupied by Wheatons, the booksellers and stationers. In recent years, remaining tram lines have been unearthed during road works.

The first electric tram driven by the Mayor, 1905. The Mayor, Councillor C. Perry, was to drive the first electric tram on 4 April. Twelve new trams were to be put into operation. Previously a horse-drawn service had operated in the city – from 1884 eight horse trams took over 400,000 people around the city – but these were now sold off. At the inauguration ceremony for the electric trams large crowds gathered outside the Guildhall as five garlanded vehicles lined up to take the local dignitaries on the first trip around Exeter.

The first trams are seen making their way up High Street with the street lined with hundreds of people, 1905. The front tram is just outside the entrance to the Eastgate Arcade. Spectators watch from the window of the Cathedral Dairy and from Boons the butcher's. The procession was led by a flag-bedecked horse tram saying its last farewells. It went as far as the London Inn Square, and then returned to the old depot in New North Road.

Exeter Corporation Tram, *c.* 1905. The Exeter tram system was to consist of twelve trams which cost £7,000. New track and paving were to be laid, overhead equipment fitted and a depot and generating plant built. The total cost was £584,000. The trams were double-deckers holding fifty-four persons. Each vehicle was powered by two 25 hp motors and weighed 8½ tons.

A further extension of the tram lines created another cause for celebration. In 1906 a new track was opened to Alphington, and again the Mayor was asked to drive this vehicle. The Alphington Road tram bears the city's coat of arms and is filled with special guests. It is followed by another decorated tram. The vehicles are almost off the new bridge that had opened in 1905, with huge crowds hemming them in. On the left is seen the premises of S. Randall, the well-known Exeter seed merchants. A stout policeman is keeping control, although most heads are turned to watch the photographer.

The new Exe Bridge is shown here shortly after completion, *c.* 1906, but at this time the new Alphington line has not been laid. On each end of the bridge were lamps, while the large central poles on each side were designed as traction poles for the new trams and were an integral part of the bridge design. Behind the tram is shown Howards Commercial Hotel, advertising 'well aired beds'. At this time the roads of Alphingon Street (left) Cowick Street (centre) and Okehampton Street (right) are clearly defined. All buildings shown no longer exist and the bridge has been demolished.

Still to be seen on the Crediton road into Exeter the 4½ ton bronze statue of General Redvers Buller was unveiled on 6 September 1906. Made by Mr Burton of Ditton, the equestrian statue of a charger faces into Exeter. The statue was paid for by a shilling fund, with donations coming from all over the world. Some contributors, however, were very displeased that the statue would face away from the General's home town of Crediton and suggested that it should be reversed. This did not come to pass.

The steepness of Fore Street has often led to traffic problems including accidents. On 25 April 1906 a traction engine pulling a wagon of bricks got into trouble halfway up Fore Street, when its load overturned. This attracted a great deal of attention from visitors to Walter Otton the ironmongers, who are seen crowding around the steaming traction engine.

Today marathon racing in Exeter is a popular pastime, and has become a major annual event. This photograph, taken on 3 April 1909 of the West of England Marathon Race, could be the earliest record of a marathon race ever recorded in Exeter. An enthusiastic crowd cheers on number 18 who is just about to pass the Guildhall. Outside, a child holding a hoop and stick looks on with fascination. The runner is accompanied by two men on bicycles.

Fore Street, *c.* 1910. Traditionally Fore Street has been the home of numerous trades and was a busy thoroughfare into the city. The top of Fore Street had some interesting buildings including the Lower Market, the Lounge Cinema and latterly the Chevalier Inn, shown left and occupied by C. Ham, wine and spirit merchant, and Martin's Bookshop. In the 1920s 78 and 79 Fore Street were threatened with demolition by Woolworths, who tried to buy the site. The buildings were some of the best historical premises in the city. Such was the opposition that both were saved – but sadly they were destroyed in the 1942 blitz.

Exe Bridge and promenade, *c.* 1910. The arrival of the new Exe Bridge was also to be responsible for changes to the areas immediately adjacent to the river. As the bridge was completed riverside properties were removed, and a new riverside walkway was created at Shooting Marsh Style. A new stone wall and bollards together with tree planting gave a new look to the edge of the river. At a slightly later date this side of the river provided rented boats, approached by wooden steps attached to the wall. Riverside leisure became popular.

The Quay, *c.* 1910. The Quay at Exeter was substantially developed in Elizabethan times and was constructed in conjunction with the Exeter Ship Canal. A ferry has crossed the river at this point from 1641, and in latter times has operated with a wire across the river. In 1835 two substantial warehouses were built for the storage of goods. Two horses are pulling a wagon up the Quay and would have made their way to Quay Hill, a steep incline up to Coombe Street and the city centre.

Exeter's Cattle Market occupied a substantial site on the banks of the River Exe adjacent to Bonhay Road and a very short distance from the old Exe Bridge built in 1905. The location allowed stock to be moved into the city without actually coming into the city centre, which would have been common practice in earlier times. This portrait of *c.* 1910 is a classic study of a bowler-hatted Devon shepherd who would have walked his stock to market. He may then have taken advantage of the nearby taverns and inns in Bonhay Road: a favourite would have been the Star and Garter.

West Street, *c.* 1910. At the beginning of this century the area of West Street was one of the poorest in the city, but it contained a strong community spirit. Many of the residents worked in industries nearby. In early times merchants had been attracted to the area, and some fine timber buildings still existed but in poor condition. Life was hard for some families and often the children's playground was the street. The view looking down West Street shows its continuation to meet Coombe Street and the top of Quay Hill. The road boundary was the railed City Wall.

Exeter Quay, *c.* 1910. This excellent view of Exeter Quay is taken from opposite Colleton Hill and clearly shows the red sandstone cliff which created the ideal situation for a Quay. On the right can be seen a number of buildings used for commercial purposes. Clearly shown is a large quantity of scrap metal used as ballast in ships. Beyond, cellars pierce the cliff face to a depth of 90 ft; they were to prove ideal for storage. Above is the impressive Colleton Cresent built from 1802 to 1814 by Matthew Nosworthy. Previously this site had been a rackfield for drying cloth. At the end of the Quay are the warehouses, transit shed and Custom House. Virtually no building on the skyline exists today, except the church (left) St Michaels and All Angels and (right) Colleton Crescent.

Ship at the basin, *c.* 1910. The provision of better offloading facilities for ships was seen to be a valuable asset that would complete the construction of the Exeter Ship Canal. Using some waste ground a basin was constructed at the head of the Canal and removed the necessity for shipping to enter the river. The basin was duly opened by the Mayor and councillors on Michaelmas Day 1830. Hundreds of people came to welcome the first vessel to enter the basin – *The Ranger*, with colours and flags flying. It was a memorable sight and the beginning of a new era for Exeter. The photograph shows the head of the basin with a vessel of foreign origin moored at the 1830 warehouses.

Shipping at Kings Arms Sluice, *c.* 1900. Seagoing ships wanting to use the Port of Exeter would enter the Exeter Ship Canal at Turf and make their way up to the Quay right at the heart of the city. Towing horses were used to pull the vessels along the canal, as were steam tugs. If necessary, the vessels could moor at the pounds at several points on the canal. Stables also existed along the route, for the horses. These vessels are probably waiting to moor at the Quay. The water level for the canal is carefully controlled at this point, and the gates remain closed if the river water level is high.

The Higher Leat, *c.* 1910. Since early times Exeter has used the resources of the River Exe to power its mills. A number of industries were to place themselves in close proximity to water and sometimes the leats were covered, flowing underneath buildings. Tremlett's Tannery in Edmund Street was built between two leats and the company's trademark was often its smell, which could float up into the city centre. Dozens of hides were cleaned in sheds in Commercial Road. Our view shows the Higher Leat at Leat Terrace, with Tremlett's Tannery in the background.

Workers at Parkins, Exe Island. Among the well-known industrial businesses in Exeter, Messrs Parkins of Exe Island, established in the 1850s, have a long-standing reputation. The company occupied an extensive site on the area of Exe Island adjacent to Bonhay Road and Tudor Street. The company had a long relationship with the area and many of their workers would have come from the immediate vicinity. Here we have a fine photograph of bowler-hatted and capped staff. They are sitting with a large pile of scrap iron at their feet. Much of the company's work involved the use of foundries making large numbers of products in iron and steel. They were also stockists of other products. A small trade catalogue advertises the following products from the Bonhay and Eagle Foundries on Exe Island: bar iron, bellows, bolts, chain, coach ironworks, screws, cotter pins, files and rasps, furnace pans, corrugated sheets, grindstones, horse shoes and nails, coopers hoops, nails, rain-water goods, springs – and so on.

In 1911 the *Daily Mail* instigated an Around Britain Air Race with a prize of £10,000. One of the competitors was to be the famous Colonel Cody. A staging post for the race was to be in fields at Whipton and Colonel Cody arrived here on 27 July 1911. It was said that his plane was given the name 'The Cathedral' because of its unusual construction. His next stop was to be Salisbury.

The opening of Rougemont Gardens, 1912. In 1768 John Patch, Surgeon of Exeter, purchased a run-down site adjacent to Rougemont Castle. The grounds formed part of what was once the castle moat. In 1770 he constructed a fine house which today is known as Rougemont House. The property was in private hands until the turn of the century; in 1911 it was purchased by the city. The beautiful grounds were duly opened to the public on 2 April 1912. The property was opened by the Mayor, accompanied by the Mace Sergeants bearing their silver gilt maces. Reporters are eagerly taking notes.

The top of Fore Street at St Olave's Church. The vast majority of buildings shown here were destroyed in the last war. As one passed up the street an impressive variety of buildings led to the city centre. The street was the same width from Fore Street to Sidwell Street. Today upper High Street is 50 per cent wider and the pre-war character has been lost. Fore Street still retains numerous interesting buildings in its lower reaches, and greater enthusiasm is being shown in restoring character back into the street.

New Bridge Street, *c.* 1915. The entry of Commercial Road is on the right, leading to the riverside and Quay after passing through an industrial area. The West Quarter was also approached from Edmund Street. On the left of the photograph is the corner of Bonhay Road, which led to the old Cattle Market. It had a prominent site overlooking the river. On the corner of Bonhay Road was the Star and Garter pub. A short distance up New Bridge Street was the former premises of Pinder and Tuckwell, at this time acting as shipping agents to all parts of the world. A mix of traffic is seen using the street, which was constructed in the 1770s: vehicles include a tram, covered wagons and handcarts.

The River Exe freezes, *c.* 1917. On occasions the Exe has frozen almost solid. Here a winter scene shows locals walking on the frozen river. Such scenes at Exeter are rare as the climate is generally mild. Although this image is not dated, other photographs suggest it was taken in February 1917. The people in the front are standing on the wooden platform, used by leisure boats which operated below Commercial Road.

One of Exeter's most talked-about crashes took place dramatically in the middle of Exe Bridge on 7 March 1917. The vehicle ran away in Fore Street and hurtled down the street with the driver unable to stop it. It finally overturned in the middle of Exe Bridge, with a tragic loss of lives. The photographer Henry Wykes, whose studio overlooked the bridge (in the building shown behind the overturned tram), quickly took his camera and recorded the event. Only two photographs of the incident are known to exist.

Exeter Quay, *c.* 1920. Exeter's fine Quayside warehouses are shown in their original state with the buildings separated by a yard with gates. By the middle of this century the Port of Exeter was at the end of its working life. At the turn of the century, approximately three hundred vessels annually would have used Exeter Ship Canal to arrive at the Quay. The most important products were petroleum, coal, timber, cement and sugar. One of the most remembered imports to come into Exeter was French onions: they were apparently stored in the warehouses and sold around Exeter by bicycle.

The transit shed and the Quay. Taken from Haven Banks, this family photograph shows the transit shed on the Quay in its original state as a working building. The shed was extended towards the Custom House and used to store fresh fish on ice. This practice gave rise to its local name of the Fish Quay. During the renovation of the building in recent times the extension was demolished and the building brought back to its original size. Most of the buildings shown in the background have now been demolished. The City Wall is seen left.

The Custom House and Quay, *c.* 1920. This shows the Custom House at Exeter when it was a working building. Customs and Excise operated from the building for over 300 years before departing in 1989. It is recognised as probably the earliest brick building in Exeter, and on its first floor boasts one of the most important decorated plaster ceilings in the south-west. Originally the front arcading was open. The transit shed is seen on the right and above it the line of the city wall which arrives at the back of the Custom House. The building below the city wall (right), is the Custom House Inn, which was demolished when the city wall fell on it in 1927.

Boating on the Exe, *c.* 1920. After the turn of the century the popularity of boating was to increase. Here we see a large group of people undertaking a cruise down the Exe. The journey would probably include the Exeter Ship Canal as the river course was limited by Trews weir. The vessels are leaving from beside Exe Bridge, where a landing platform extended out into the river. Between the two buildings in the background was the entrance to a leat which divided the area known as Shilhay. The leat entered the Exe again at Quay Bridge. Cottages and the Malt House are seen on the right at the rear.

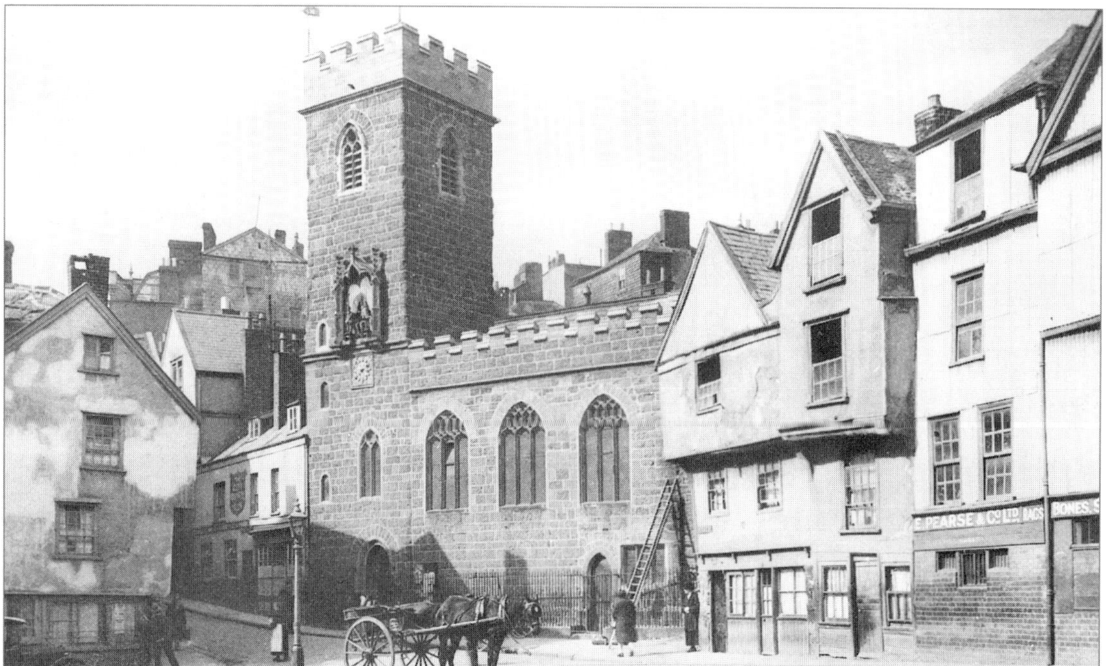

St Mary Steps and old houses, *c.* 1910. The building shown on the left, probably dating from the fifteenth century, was to be demolished in the 1930s, and the site was left empty for a number of years. At this time the Kings Arms Inn was next to the church. The railings in front of the church were removed during the Second World War. The two dilapidated sixteenth-century buildings (centre) were to be restored in the 1930s. The two buildings (right) are shown bricked up and grilled. The properties were used by E. Pearse & Co., rag, bone and skin merchants. This company was well known in the West Quarter.

A depot for the new electric trams was constructed at the junction of Paris Street with Heavitree Road and was originally designed to hold sixteen trams. This photograph shows four trams which are advertising local companies: Colson & Co, Paish & Co. Pianos, and the Cathedral Dairy in High Street. The depot continued in use long after the demise of the trams and housed the city's buses. Today the site is a block of flats for the elderly.

Tram no. 32 is operating in Heavitree Road just outside the tram depot. One of the first new tram routes was to be from the Guildhall to Heavitree Road (Livery Dole). This particular route was quickly extended and eventually went to the top of East Wonford Hill, with access over the new bridge to the foot of Dunsford Hill.

Sidwell Street, *c.* 1920. This particularly fine record shows Sidwell Street as an interesting and busy thoroughfare. Numerous small businesses were found in this street and also some buildings of note. Many of these properties existed after the last war but the street was to be destroyed and rebuilt. Here we see two city trams in action with the conductor of the front vehicle attending to some problem with his passengers. The fashion for blinds drawn out over the pavement was one of the features of shopping in Exeter.

1920–1939

High Street looking down from Queen Street, late 1930s. At the junction with Queen Street, High Street had an interesting line of façades that extended to Goldsmith Street. The retailers consisted of Lennard's boots and shoes, H. Samuel, jewellers, and the large premises of Waltons, a popular Exeter store that closed in 1975. Other attractive shopfronts existed in Goldsmith Street and at the top of Queen Street. With the development of the site for Marks & Spencer in the 1970s all these buildings were pulled down. Some elements of past architectural style were introduced to placate the situation.

The junction of Queen Street and High Street, seen here in the 1920s, was always a busy place, especially as there was two-way traffic. On a crowded day a policeman is on duty in the middle of the road. This was a common practice. Officers on the beat would be well known to citizens, and life was conducted in a friendly and understanding manner. The officers were held in great respect.

Traffic jams in High Street, *c.* 1920. This shows clearly why police officers were needed to direct traffic in High Street. There appears to be a blockage at Queen Street and the police officer is trying to sort out the problem. The traffic is stopped outside Colsons. Frost's Hairdressing Salon (left) is offering manicures, massage and chiropody.

The Exeter City war memorial in Northernhay Gardens is without doubt one of the finest memorials in the country. The commission for this prestigious work was given to John Angel who had lived in Exeter as a child. The 31ft high monument is surrounded by four magnificent bronzes at its base – a nurse, prisoner of war, soldier and sailor. At its summit Victory stands triumphant with her foot on the body of a slain dragon and holds high a spray of laurel. The memorial was unveiled by the Right Honourable Admiral David Beatty on 24 July 1923.

Maudes Motor Mart, *c.* 1920. For those wanting a new car this garage in Paris Street offered great value! A range of Clyno cars is on offer, from £162 10*s* to £245 for a deluxe version.

The corner of Bedford Street before rebuilding, *c.* 1920. The customers are looking in the window of Depree and Young, jewellers and specialists in silver. A sign above the window points the way to Bedford Circus.

Dellers Café, Bedford Street, *c.* 1930. At the turn of the century no one would have guessed that one of the most important centres for the city's social life was soon to be built. In 1912 Lloyds Bank built a single-storey bank on the corner of High Street and Bedford Street. Dellers, originating in Paignton, constructed a huge building above and beside the bank. Its entrance stood in Bedford Street. The interior was opulent and grand and was to become a mecca for local people. No other building in Exeter this century has evoked such memories as Dellers Café.

Dellers dining room. Deller's Café was capable of dealing with any kind of function, having a number of large function areas. Here one room is laid out to accommodate about two hundred people for dinner. The room is decorated with sumptuous relief plasterwork friezes and an elaborate cornice. The wood-block floor made the room suitable for balls, tea dances and other activities. Fancy dress balls were very popular.

Before the war no other business in Exeter offered better facilities for parties, balls, dinner dances and whist drives than Dellers Café. Situated right in the heart of the city on the corner of High Street and Bedford Street, it was the perfect place for pre-show dinners and drinks before going to the Theatre Royal. Here two ladies have prepared themselves for a big fancy dress occasion – and had their photographs taken as a souvenir.

Dellers interior, *c.* 1920. The first to sample Dellers Café were soldiers, despite the fact that the building was not quite finished; however, the ceremony went ahead on 5 December 1916. A new era had begun! The interior of Dellers was lavish and its centre of attraction was a two-tiered dining room complete with palm court orchestra. Its balconies were decorated with relief plasterwork with classical cherubs. The capitals of its pillars were also undertaken in reliefs. The walls were panelled in wood, and built into the first balcony there were a number of discreet curtained alcoves for private meetings. A fine staircase also led into the dining room, and was used with effect by singers and entertainers.

The massively built Heavitree-stone Bampfylde House, seen here in about 1930, was one of the city's museums. Built in the late sixteenth century and situated on the corner of Bampfylde Street and Catherine Street, the property was originally the town house of the Bampfylde family, and was sold to Arthur Guest in 1929.

Bampfylde House interior, the Oak Room. The property was restored by Mr Guest, businessman and City Councillor, who in turn let it out to an antique dealer: it was accordingly furnished in period style. In 1934 Guest sold the house to the City, and it was opened as a museum (seen here, in the year of its opening). Bampfylde House had a fascinating history and was a particularly fine property. However, it was severely damaged in the blitz of May 1942 and its remains were demolished.

The Theatre Royal, *c.* 1930. This was the hub of the city's entertainment and stood at the junction of New North Road and Longbrook Street. The building had one of the most interesting histories of any English theatre. Built in 1886, the theatre was to catch on fire on 5 September 1887: 186 people were burnt to death. The tragedy was to bring in legislation for the introduction of the fire curtain in all English theatres. Further tragedy transpired when the theatre was demolished in 1963, bringing to an end an ancient tradition in the heart of the city.

Publicity stunt at the Theatre Royal, *c.* 1930. Of all the buildings in Exeter that could effectively pull off publicity stunts the Theatre Royal, at the junction of New North Road and Longbrook Street, was well equipped. A classic scene is set up outside the theatre using a visiting actress (unknown) to promote a new fleet of Vauxhall cars. The star's vehicle, however, is in miniature. The manager of the Theatre Royal looks on.

Local historians and archaeologists, *c.* 1930. Exeter has always attracted the attention of historians and archaeologists, and in this century two early and important pioneers were Ethel Lega Weekes and Arthur Everett. The couple are engrossed in viewing the fabric of an ancient building – which could be St Katherine's Priory. The pair made important contributions to the history of the city. Miss Weekes, a fellow of the Royal Historical Society, concentrated on historical matters, while self-taught Arthur Everett specialised in archaeological aspects. Mr Everett conducted numerous digs between the two world wars and was highly respected. Among the works produced by Miss Weekes was *The Topography of the Cathedral Close*. She died in 1949 aged eighty-five and Arthur Everett in 1979 at the age of ninety. Arthur learnt much about Exeter while driving trams through the streets of the city.

Willey's, 1930s. Many people in Exeter will be familiar with Willey's, who operated in Water Lane. The company specialised in gas appliances and was at one time the city's biggest employers. Its most famous product was the slot gas meter: there was a special meter factory in Willeys Avenue. Some very large appliances were also made by the company, which was skilled in foundry work. The company had a very progressive outlook and was responsible for the erection of the Trews Weir Suspension Bridge across the River Exe, giving its workers better access to work. The photograph shows moulding work under way.

Willey's advertisement.

The Bedford Garage, *c.* 1930. In the very centre of pre-war Exeter stood this huge covered garage. It was adjacent to St John's School, and the western side of the garage backed on to the rear of Bedford Circus. It was entered from either Catherine Street or Bampfylde Street. Not only did the garage undertake sales of vehicles but it offered the most convenient parking in Exeter. The garage was destroyed in 1942. The new Princesshay was to have a garage – Hughes of Exeter.

For many Exonians the loss of the Exeter trams was a sad event. With the advent of double-decker buses many of the tram rails were to be ripped up or asphalted over. The traction poles were turned into lamps. Some of the trams were scrapped but others were sold to corporations elsewhere. On 19 August 1931 Mayor C. Perry took over tram no. 14 which, with flags flying, toured areas of the city where the overhead lines still existed. At the end of the journey the tram entered the depot and the power was switched off: the last tram had been put to rest.

One of Exeter's most impressive processions took place on 25 June 1933 when the 800th anniversary of the founding of Exeter Cathedral was marked. A large procession of mayors from Devon, Somerset, Cornwall and Dorset joined the celebrations. The procession is seen leaving the west front of the Cathedral watched by hundreds of people. Exeter's Mayor, K. Gatey MC, is seen at the head with the Mace Sergeants carrying the city's regalia, the sword of Henry VII and the Cap of Maintenance. Each preceding Mayor is also flanked by Mace Sergeants. The whole colourful scene is recorded by a man using a handcranked ciné camera. To the right is the end of the demolished St Mary Major's Church. Based around a week's celebration, from 24 June to 2 July, the procession was the highlight of the event. At 11.30 am the Lord Bishop of Liverpool included in the service a sermon, matins and choral works.

Today at the top of South Street stands a ruin, left as a memorial to the Second World War. It is the remains of the hall of the Vicars Choral, a group of buildings dating from the late 1400s that stood opposite the west front of Exeter Cathedral. Known as the College, it provided accommodation for priests, consisting of two rows of cottages and a communal hall. The college had an impressive entrance at the eastern end. By the end of the 1900s the College had been removed, with only the hall (which had been altered in the sixteenth century) remaining. It remained intact, as seen in this photograph until the Second World War, when it was blitzed.

St John's School, *c.* 1935. Before the Second World War St John's School occupied the site of today's Princesshay. Walking up the precinct today you are actually walking up the playground. The original school had stood in the High Street but was demolished in about 1880. New school buildings were placed just back from the High Street: the entrance was through an archway on which stood two 'blue boys', the symbol of the school. The school was blitzed in 1942.

Queen Street, *c.* 1935. The creation of Queen Street in the 1830s was to provide the city with some fine architecture and much of it is still retained today. However, a major calamity took place in the 1970s when the street was destroyed at its most sensitive point, the junction with High Street. In 1850 a group of buildings was constructed to look as one but allowing a variety of trades to flourish. In style and sensitivity it suited the location well. Its well-designed rounded corner entered High Street and did not jar against older buildings. Our photograph shows the building intact, except for an inappropriate change to the centre section. It led to the *Express and Echo Western Times* and *Exeter Gazette* Printing Works. Boots the Chemists occupied the corner site at this time. This elegant façade was torn down in the late 1970s and replaced by today's C & A building. It was one of the worst decisions in the postwar history of Exeter, and provoked outrage from many citizens.

Lower High Street, *c.* 1935. Properties in Exeter's High Street had much more character than they do today. Each shopfront was individual. In many respects modern retailing has not taken sufficient notice of this, producing shopfronts which are unsuitable for the premises. Our photograph shows, to the left, Cornishes on their corner site. High Street starts with Hepworth's the tailors and next door Woodley's Shoes followed by Garton and King, domestic and sanitary engineers. Their foundry was at the rear in Waterbeer Street. Pinder and Tuckwell offered 'real tailoring', and Moon and Sons some of the best pianos in Exeter. No. 193 was occupied by Gilbey's wine and spirits.

The London Inn Square was at the junction of High Street and Sidwell Street, and was a focal point in the city. It took its name from the large hotel that had been on the site since coaching days, from which travellers went to and from London. Many people in the area were involved in the coaching industry. The New London Hotel was one of Exeter's oldest coaching establishments but was to be removed for the building of the Savoy Cinema, which opened in 1936. At the rear of the Square is the Theatre Royal: the hotel would have been a popular rendezvous before going on to enjoy the local entertainment.

Upper High Street, late 1930s. The photograph was taken from the entrance to the London Inn Square: the entrance to the Eastgate Arcade is clearly shown on the left, with a sign above the arched entrance. The clock states it is nearly 8.30 a.m. Built in the 1880s, the arcade offered some exclusive shopping. The National Provincial Bank formed part of the entrance, and next door was the substantial post office building.

Central High Street and St Lawrence's Church, late 1930s. The north side of High Street, once the site of one of Exeter's most ancient churches, St Lawrence's is now occupied by Lloyds Bank and other retailers. The entrance to Bedford Street is on the left, with the rounded corner of Dellers Café above the ground floor entrance of Lloyds Bank.

The Eastgate Arcade took its name from the site of the city's main gate demolished in 1784. In 1882 a fine glass-roofed arcade was built to attract quality shopping. The arcade was regularly decorated with floral displays to add to its ambience. The main entrance into High Street had two large wrought-iron gates which were closed at the end of the day. The main feature of the Arcade was its splendid round stained-glass window at the southern end. In 1939 twenty-four businesses operated from the arcade. This photograph shows the Eastgate Arcade after being decorated for the Silver Jubilee of King George V and Queen Mary on 6 May 1935. The contract for decorating was given to Prince's Nurseries of St Thomas.

Bedford Circus, *c.* 1938. Pre-war Exeter had two prime focal points, the Cathedral and Bedford Circus. Bedford Circus, built by Robert Stribling between 1773 and 1826, consisted of twenty-seven properties and a chapel. It was recognised as one of the finest Regency crescents in England: originally private dwellings, with a communal oval garden, the Circus became the centre for prestigious businesses in Exeter. Today such an architectural feature would be a major attraction. Bedford Circus was bombed on 4 May 1942 but a large portion remained, still standing but gutted: this included the Chapel. The City Council demolished all standing remains. An opportunity to rebuild the Circus was lost and in its place new buildings were created which in no way compared with the famous Circus.

The Higher Market, Queen Street, 1938. Designed by George Dymond, the Higher Market was opened for business on 24 July 1838. This photograph was taken 100 years later. The Higher Market has totally dominated the top of Queen Street, and was to become a fundamental part of the city's life. Traders would come to sell meat, fish, flowers, vegetables and second-hand goods in the open halls. Country people came into Exeter every Friday to sell their wares at a rate of perhaps 4,000 people a day at peak times. In 1938 Greenslade's Tours operated from a closed section of the market, offering coach tours of the region.

CHEMISTS.
ROSS' TAILORS
J.LYONS & Co LTD

Exeter High Street, *c.* 1938. Before the war the northern side of Exeter's High Street boasted some of the finest buildings in the city. No. 226 (second left) was the offices of the *Western Morning News* and the *Express and Echo*, and dated from the sixteenth century. Its neighbour, no. 227, was the premises of the tailors J. & G. Ross. Thc central building with two projecting bay windows is a mock-up of a historic property. No. 229 was tragically deliberately destroyed by the Saxone Shoe Company in the early 1930s: its fine Jacobean interior was exported to America and is now in a museum. The façade was rebuilt with windows from a property demolished in North Street. The Midland Bank seen on the right was to be demolished and rebuilt after the war.

The Commercial Union and other buildings in High Street. Central High Street contained some of Exeter's most interesting buildings. This was certainly the case from 238 to 247 High Street. The group consisted of the Commercial Union building constructed in a Classical style with Corinthian columns and topped by a statue of King Alfred. William Brufords next door was one of Exeter's finest jewellers and still operates today. Its famous 'Old Father Time' clock was a feature in the High Street. Fred Ford Signs at no. 242 also gave office space to the Exeter and County Club for gentlemen. The double-gabled, black and white building was occupied by Wippel Bros & Row ironmongers, one of Exeter's oldest businesses. The Devon and Somerset stores, British Shoe Company and St Lawrence's Church complete a fascinating group.

High Street at Eastgate, late 1930s. Taken just in front of the Eastgate Arcade, this photograph shows, on the right, the premises of Mark Rowe & Sons, 266 High Street. The building was constructed from stone taken from the demolished Eastgate, which was removed in 1784. A bronze plaque is fixed on the side of the building giving the history of the Eastgate. The plaque can now be seen attached to a granite plinth in High Street. It will be noticed that a figure is shown in an alcove on the façade: this is the original figure of Henry VII which was taken from the actual gate when it was removed. Unfortunately this precious statue was destroyed in the Exeter blitz of 1942.

High Street at St Stephen's Church, late 1930s. The High Street is shown as a two-way traffic system under the cautious eye of a police officer. Outside St Stephen's Church a tram traction pole is used for a sign indicating 'Public Swimming Baths Hot Water' and YMCA opposite. The baths operated by the City Council were situated at the end of King's Alley. The four-storeyed building shown on the right was famous for its magnificent plaster ceiling, the Apollo Ceiling: it was a local attraction and could be visited at no charge. The building at this time was used by Bobby & Co. Ltd. Dellers Café was next door.

Exeter High Street, *c.* 1938. Before the Second World War two buildings stood on the corner of High Street and South Street, but they were blitzed in 1942. One property was Holman and Ham, the chemists. A tram traction pole is seen on the corner with a traffic light attached: this was a new push-button system for pedestrians, which was warily used. Next to the chemists was the Fifty Shilling Tailors. Gents' suits are advertised for 37*s* 6*d*. A shoe shop operates next door under the name of Dicks. The statue of St Peter is just visible on the left overlooking High Street, and a sign states 'St Peter's Corner'.

The Cathedral Close, *c.* 1939. Unlike today, parking in the Cathedral Close did not present a problem. Here we see vehicles parked outside the famous building known as Mol's Coffee House. The railings surrounding the Cathedral Close have been removed to help the war effort and the Close is now an open space: a dwarf wall was later constructed. No. 1 Catherine Street is occupied by the Cathedral Art Gallery, whose first owner was the artist John Shapland, a prolific painter. Worth & Co., picture framers and restorers, operated from Mol's and a dilapidated sign above the front door states that the first floor room was where the sea captains met with Sir Francis Drake to plot against the Spanish Armada. The property next door is owned by Irene's, costumier, and her neighbour is the tailors – Henson's.

Bedford Street, looking towards High Street from the junction with Catherine Street, 1939. Underground toilets were built in the middle of the street and a fine lamp positioned nearby. The new corner building was now occupied by The Constitutional Club and by Trumps who sold silks, gowns, hats, flowers and fruit. Barclay's Bank had taken the prominent site facing the High Street.

Jourdan's Box Factory, Sidwell Street, 1939. The building shown stood nearly opposite today's Odeon Cinema. Mr G.A. Jourdan, a box and packaging specialist, came to Exeter to protect his business just before the Second World War. Purchasing this building, Mr Jourdan felt he was safe; however, the site was to be bombed. Jourdan's acquired a new site in Whipton and still operates today, employing a large number of people.

The Chevalier Inn, Fore Street, 1940. In the first half of this century most people in Exeter would have known the Chevalier House at the top of Fore Street with its famous equestrian ridge tile. Nos 78 and 79 Fore Street were built in the seventeenth century and from 1940 became the Chevalier Inn. Both buildings were classified with the highest architectural merit but narrowly escaped demolition in 1929. The restored buildings shown here in 1940 had a short life of two years, being blitzed in May 1942.

1939–1942

A view to the Cathedral across South Street. A narrow street before the war, South Street was to sustain severe losses. On its eastern side a fine row of buildings with elegant façades collapsed during the bombing. Only half the street was left standing. This view, taken through an archway near Milk Street, shows Exeter's most famous building still standing. The ruin at its base is the destroyed Hall of the Vicars Choral, one of Exeter's historical gems. A later entrance to the Hall was from South Street; the ruin was retained as a memorial. A Saxon doorway from St George's Church, South Street, was saved and placed in the ruin, where it remains today.

Exeter's Home Guard, seen here in 1941, was to consist of approximately two thousand men. Those who joined up were not fit or too old for normal duty, or were in reserved occupations. The Home Guard in Exeter ran from 1940 to 1944, and operated from a base in Pancras Lane in the centre of the city; the Higher Market was used for practice in adverse weather conditions. Other indoor sessions took place in the school house in Paul Street.

The bombing of Exeter, May 1942. This remarkable photograph is one of two images of the bombing of Exeter on 4 May 1942. The photograph was taken with a folding Kodak camera by someone who was in the Rougemont Hotel on the night of the bombing. As the bombs fell this photograph was taken from the top of the building. The Cathedral is seen beneath huge smoke clouds, and in front of the building is the spire of St Mary Major's Church.

Fire appliances in High Street, 4 May 1942. Firefighters had more than their fair share of work as Exeter literally caught fire after the dropping of 10,000 incendiary bombs combined with high explosives. Manpower was not adequate as the city reeled from the onslaught. One building after another was lost because of fire. A further element was a north-east wind, which fanned flames across the city. Here firefighters desperately try to save Colson's in High Street.

The Globe Hotel, 4 May 1942. A fine hotel stood in the corner of the Cathedral Yard leading to South Street. On its south side was Little Stile, one of the ancient gateways to the Close. The Globe Hotel had origins going back to the seventeenth century and was a mix of buildings of different ages. Its location was one of the most prominent in Exeter. The Globe Hotel was gutted in 1942, as there were insufficient firefighters to save it.

The destruction of South Street, 4 May 1942. The Headmaster of the Cathedral Choristers' School left a remarkable legacy of the Exeter Blitz. An album of negatives fifty years old contained scenes never seen before. One of these is shown here. This photograph was carefully printed and showed a view from South Street looking across a destroyed Milk Street to the Lower Market at the top of Fore Street. The Italian-style tower is clearly seen.

The Cathedral in the midst of destruction, after 4 May 1942. The impact of this image has come to be recognised in postwar years as a poignant record of Exeter's survival from the Second World War. Exeter's Phoenix or Blitz fountain bears this image as its symbol. A massive high-explosive bomb was to create a hole big enough for a double-decker bus, and destroyed some of Exeter's finest buildings in the Close. The Cathedral was also hit on its south side, with St James's Chapel being destroyed. There was severe internal damage but the majority of the building survived intact.

In Upper High Street close to the Eastgate Arcade was the General Post Office. The three-storeyed Victorian building, constructed in 1885, was still partially standing after the raid of May 1942. Its two arched doorways are seen and most of the façade. Adjacent to it is a large empty space, the site of the lost Eastgate Arcade. It was to be destroyed as a huge fireball swept up its full length, also destroying buildings at the rear at the top of Southernhay.

The devastated High Street, 5 May 1942. The morning after the main air raid of 4 May the central area of Exeter lay smashed. Buildings had collapsed into the street, caught fire, and many had been utterly destroyed. The air was full of a thick acrid smoke, choking those who tried to save the remaining city. Red hot brick blocked the path of rescuers and the area was to smoulder for days. The smell was one that was to linger with many citizens for a lifetime. The view shows the High Street taken from the remains of the post office. St Lawrence's Church is still standing.

The Commercial Union, High Street. Gradually the central area of the city was cleared, with remaining structures being removed. The Commercial Union building stood uneasily among the devastation awaiting its fate. No other building would be built in this style again in Exeter. The company was to remove its symbol (King Alfred) from its lofty perch and retain it for posterity. Only its head appears to have survived, however.

Upper High Street after May 1942. The destruction of Upper High Street was considerable but not all buildings were totally lost although many were gutted. L.H. Fearis at the corner of Paris Street still stood and other properties at the top of Southernhay East, including the Exeter Gaslight and Coke Co. Ltd. The photograph is taken from where the Mark Rowe building stood, and on the left can be seen old Paris Street. It was much narrower than today: changes were to be made to the road pattern during the rebuilding.

LIMITED
TO CAR PARK
PUBLIC LAVATORIES

Dellers Café still stood on its prominent corner site after May 1942, but was gutted. It is suggested that incendiaries set the kitchen on fire and destroyed the interior. Travelling fires from Bobby's are also linked to its fate. The magnificent decorated entrance to Dellers is seen in Bedford Street. The structure was so well built that it is said there was difficulty in demolishing it. Reconstruction could have been a feasible alternative, but the building was pulled down.

On 8 May 1942 the King and Queen arrived at Exeter to inspect the war damage. They visited bombed towns and cities to boost the morale of subjects. A meeting took place with Mr Herbert Read who was to be responsible for some remarkable restoration of the Cathedral's fabric. The Royals also had a tour of the city.

Bedford Circus, after May 1942. One of the most contentious decisions about the rebuilding of Exeter was the failure to recreate Bedford Circus. On entering Bedford Circus from High Street, on the right was a Savings Bank: during the blitz of 4 May fire guards took cover in the basement, but lost their lives after a high explosive bomb fell. The Circus was gutted and partially destroyed. About a third was to remain, but all was pulled down.

The Lower Market, *c.* 1943. Designed in 1833 by Charles Fowler, the Lower Market at the top of Fore Street was also to be gutted. Its architectural style was quite unique in Exeter and probably in the south-west. It too was to be demolished as an unsafe structure, and was replaced by St George's Market.

The demolition of standing buildings in High Street. Practically the whole shell of Dellers Café and Lloyds Bank had survived but were to be pulled down. The ancient church of St Lawrence was gutted, but was to be demolished. One of the city's finest classical façades, the Commercial Union, still retained its famous statue of King Alfred and its fine Corinthian columns. The whole façade was removed.

Ernest Fraser, Police Sergeant no. 56, was awarded a medal for bravery for the actions he took to save life during the Exeter Blitz on 4 May 1942. He also received a certificate stating that 'By the King's Order the name of Ernest Fraser, Police Sergeant, Exeter City Police was published in the *London Gazette* on 9 October 1942 as commended for brave conduct in civil defence. I am charged to record high appreciation of the service rendered. Winston Churchill, Prime Minister and First Lord of the Treasury.' Ernest had been involved in a number of difficult situations but at all times was modest about his actions.

The end of the war is marked by a service in the Cathedral Close.

1945–1960

Barratt's shoe shop, High Street. Exeter's High Street has traditionally had some particularly old and interesting buildings. In 1949 a double gabled building still existed under the ownership of Barratt's. Almost opposite the premises were two of Exeter's most famous buildings – nos 226 and 227 High Street. Today only the façades of these fine seventeenth-century buildings exist, their interiors being demolished. Barratt's, however, completely removed this ancient building in the postwar period, and an opportunity to restore another part of the city's heritage was lost. The old Colson's building is shown next door; it was shortly to be demolished.

The central area, 1945. In local archives there is often a single image which epitomises a certain period in time. For Exeter, this photograph has been used to show what the enemy did to the city in the Second World War. It is important to relate, however, that this photograph shows the central area after the decision by the Local Authority to remove all the remaining standing buildings. Some of those buildings could have been saved. Deller's Café, Bedford Circus and St Lawrence's Church all fall into this category.

Temporary shops, 1948. After the bombing of Exeter a rapid decision was made that services and shops should be restored as soon as possible. One of the first initiatives was to create temporary shops, and these were duly built on the site of the Eastgate Arcade. They extended from High Street towards Southernhay and consisted of a range of flat-topped units which extended in a partial rectangle to the entrance of Southernhay East opposite the Gaslight and Coke Company. A line of dwarf-walled gardens stretched from the city wall bastion to High Street. Many Exonians will still remember this area and the shops which operated from this temporary facility.

The City Garage, New North Road, 26 October 1948. Today there are no garages in the central area of the city, and cars are gradually being eased out. In 1948 you could have filled up your car at the City Garage, which was adjacent to the Theatre Royal. Naturally the traffic was not at the level we experience today. Maude's was operating from the garage in 1948.

The latest fashions at Colson's, 1948. Ever anxious to keep ahead of fashion, one of the city's most prestigious stores, Colson's, in High Street, organised fashion shows to attract new customers. This was the ultimate look at the time.The rebuilding of the store allowed much larger retail areas for gowns and hats, and a shoe department for ladies.

The frontage of Colson's, 1949. Classified as one of Exeter's most prestigious shops, Colson's was to be completely rebuilt. At this point the remaining old building had almost been removed. New premises were to be built on the blitzed site next to St Stephen's Church. The steelwork is in place, and would soon be Wyman's bookshop. Today the entire site is used by Dingles. Colson's are still operating in this photograph, and their blinds are pulled out over the street.

Colson's frontage, 1949. The detailed architectural style of the old Colson's building added to the character of High Street. This could not be said of its replacement. Relief mouldings, fine arched windows with keystones and decorated friezes were all features of the Colson's façade. The company had at one stage integrated another earlier building into their complex, for it had a large bow window looking out over High Street. The structure had at this time been completely removed down to its foundations, and a large gap opens up a view of the Cathedral. The builder's notice shows that M.T. Sleeman and Sons are working on the building.

Clearance of sites in High Street, *c.* 1949. The central area was now being cleared for rebuilding and a large site was to be utilised by Marks & Spencer for their new store. The premises were to be constructed on the corner of Castle Street and High Street. It was to open up Castle Street which pre-war had a much narrower entrance from High Street. On the left of the photograph is shown the Savoy Cinema, and centrally, the beginning of Sidwell Street which was still intact and retained its pre-war character. The store L.H. Fearis is standing right.

Preparation of the new Marks & Spencer site, *c.* 1949. In the immediate postwar period parking was no problem in the city centre, the whole area being an open space as shown. A new spectator attraction was watching the new city take shape. Sites being developed were left with viewing areas for the public, seen right. The public are standing in Castle Street, and behind are the remains of the Westminster Bank. The large trees on the left mark the oval garden of Bedford Circus.

Beach Bros, St Thomas workshop, 1 March 1949. One of Exeter's more unusual companies is Beach Bros, which came to the city in 1940 after being ordered out of Dover by the Ministry of Production as a safer base was needed: all their original staff with their families were brought to Exeter. The company specialised in all forms of cork and timber products. Much of its early business revolved around making corks for medicine bottles, beer casks and bottled beers, although the company later expanded its business into timber products. They are still operating in Exeter today.

Regent Oil Depot, 1949. The canal was used to bring petroleum to the city, and in 1949 the Regent Oil Depot was constructed just beyond the gasworks. The area was agricultural, with allotments on each side of the canal. In latter years the land around Alphinbrook Lane was to be used for the city's industrial estate, now called Marsh Barton.

Seating up to 1,500 people, the Civic Hall in Queen Street was one of the city's prime entertainment venues. All manner of functions took place, from voting to wrestling. The Hall was created from space originally taken by butchers' stalls from the Higher Market. The original intention was that this should be a temporary measure, but it continued for many years until its closure in 1970. The photograph shows a bridal fayre or fashion show taking place in 1949. There appears to be great admiration from the audience as young brides-to-be take their pick from the latest fashions.

Miss Maude Tothill, seen here in about 1950, was associated with one of Exeter's most historic buildings, St Nicholas Priory, at the Mint in Fore Street. In 1913 the City Council, taking the advice of the Town Clerk, purchased the ancient building and restored it, and opened it to the public. The first curator was a young, enthusiastic Miss Tothill, who was curator at the Priory from 1916 to 1956. She was dedicated to the building and promoted it with huge success. One of Miss Tothill's passions was the keeping of ravens in an aviary in the grounds. When one raven called Martha died, she was preserved in a glass case and can still be seen in the Priory.

The new High Street starts to develop with the near completion of the Marks & Spencer building, 2 July 1951. A large signboard on the scaffolding states 'Marks & Spencer New Store'. The site would extend towards the London Inn Square, with other well-known companies returning to the High Street. A new street was created behind this area, 'Bailey Street' – which took its name from the bailey of Rougemont Castle.

The construction of central High Street, 1952. As part of the new redevelopment of postwar Exeter a substantial service road was to be created which would service the rear of buildings in Princesshay and the south side of High Street. The photograph is taken from the middle of the new service road, which was to be built to a considerable depth. The vehicles shown are parked on what was to become the south side of High Street but is yet to be built. The building on the left is what remains of the old Barclays Bank on the corner of Bedford Street. The scaffolding above is the roof of Lloyds Bank being built in High Street.

Bedford Street, looking towards High Street, 1952. With the removal of all buildings from the centre, road layouts were subject to change and in particular pavements and streets were widened. From the corner of Catherine Street, Bedford Street is shown to be wider than previously. On the left-hand side the site once occupied by Dellers was to become a shoe shop. The Barclays building was to be demolished and rebuilt.

Junction of High Street and Bedford Street, 1953. This was formerly the site of the famous Dellers Café.

The south side of High Street, which was once occupied by the Eastgate Arcade, National Provincial Bank, the imposing three-arched façade of the post office and a range of other buildings, was being replaced by a dominating structure, which is shown nearly complete.

The new image for Colson's is now complete, *c.* 1953; likewise, its neighbour Barratts was also rebuilt, and a very monotonous style lacking in character graces the redeveloped site. Colson's are advertising on window posters a 'Fashion and Fabric Sale'. The bookshop Wyman's is now next to St Stephen's Church: the company even operated a private library for borrowing books. Outside Colson's a tram traction pole is still being used for lighting.

Gaytons Garage, Coombe Street, 24 July 1954. Coombe Street, leading from South Street to the top of Quay Hill was an important side street but was to be truncated in the postwar period by Western Way. Overlooking this street was Central School an important provision for many local children (including the author). A flight of steps led from the street into the playground. The large tenement block called Folletts Buildings housed some of the poorer families; it was demolished to make way for new flats.

The High Street is shown nearing completion on 13 May 1955. A stark and monolithic style of architecture removed any feeling of the old city from upper High Street. The world travel service of Cook & Son had a prime central site, together with Lennards shoes and the tobacconists McGahey. The Westminster Bank had its premises above and also in Castle Street. This side street had been greatly widened. Marks & Spencer's new store was to be joined by the Scotch Wool Shop and Mark Rowe Ltd.

The High Street, 1955. This is nearly as we see it today but the corner of Bedford Street had still to be rebuilt. The shops on the south side are now operating and the traffic is starting to flow back into the central area.

Above: Bodley's Foundry, Shilhay, 1955. Bodley's Foundry, established in 1790, was one of the most specialist foundry firms in the country, producing gear wheels for industry. The massive metal cogs were made by hand. At its peak the company employed sixty to seventy workers. The industrial giants ICI recognised the skill of the Exeter company and ordered gear wheels for some of its plants in Russia. In the early years Bodley's made many products from cider presses to steam engines. When the company was sold its machinery went to the Kensington Science Museum, and the foundry became a council store.

Henry William Turner stands in front of a gear wheel, 16 August 1955.

Vulcan Signs, 1957. Many people will be familiar with the fine enamel signs that were used to promote products such as Capstan cigarettes, Woodbines, Oxo and Cadburys, but may not be aware that these signs were produced in Exeter at the Vulcan Enamel Works. The company employed 180 people, but in 1961 the factory was to close down. A merger with Willey's saved the day – but eventually both companies were forced to close.

The City Brewery, Commercial Road, 1957. The brewery had its origins in the eighteenth century. Its structure was extraordinary as it was integrated into the structure of Exeter's medieval bridge, which still existed below the road surface: the cellars used part of the arches of the old bridge. Over a period of time the brewery was to be extended. Finally it consisted of a brewhouse, store, cellars, lofts and malthouse. Behind the brewery was a shallow lake, formed by the Lower Leat before it flowed under the bridge arches and headed down Commercial Road to the Quay.

In 1957 Henry Wykes, the photographer, was commissioned to record work on the new Boots store on the corner of Northernhay Place and High Street. The photograph shows the site being prepared for the foundations. Behind the site the temporary shops which were put up in 1948 can be seen. The units extended from High Street back to Southernhay. Before the war the site was the Eastgate Arcade. Opposite them were three low gardens running in line with the ancient bastion, part of the city wall. The wall had been demolished to allow the building of Princesshay.

Boots store in High Street, 1958. In this photograph the shop is nearly completed, and features a roof-top terrace overlooking the High Street. The Plaza Cinema had stood on the site before the war, but was destroyed by a high explosive bomb. Northernhay Street used to continue in a straight line from High Street to Northernhay Gardens without interruption, but in 1951 a new street was created to act as a service road; it was Bailey Street.

1960–1980

The postwar period in Exeter was to see the final removal of some of Exeter's most ancient buildings. One could still walk in areas where it seemed that the clock had been turned back. Today such opportunities would have allowed interesting tourism development. Frog Street was a particularly old street (seen here in about 1960) and at its north end was no. 15, a timber-framed building of two storeys. Much of its interior had been preserved and the building dated from the late sixteenth century. It was destroyed in 1961 with the building of Western Way.

The police station in Waterbeer Street, early 1960s. The Victorian police station, opened in 1887, was appropriately placed at the rear of the Guildhall. Prisoners were simply taken over Waterbeer Street and straight into court. A small lane beside the conical tower, called Pancras Lane, led to Paul Street. Today only the foundation stone of the police station exists; it has been integrated into a small walled garden, and is generally overlooked by shoppers.

Coach and bus station, Paul Street, *c.* 1960. Until the 1920s Paul Street had very much its own character, with cottages and small buildings running down its northern side. A major clearance scheme created a large open site but still with properties left on its southern side. These were to be removed in the 1970s. The site became the Exeter bus and coach station until its new site became available in Paris Street. The only property to remain was a small Sunday school.

16 Goldsmith Street, 1960s. Goldsmith Street, which connected High Street to Paul Street, was a convenient and ancient city thoroughfare. Numerous small buildings ran along it and the rear of the Higher Market also came out on to the street. The rebuilding to the rear of the Guildhall in the 1970s destroyed nearly all of Goldsmith Street and drastically changed the proportions of the rear of the market.

The entrance to Exe Island, *c.* 1960. The low-lying lands from Head Weir to Exeter Quay have traditionally been the Manor of Exe Island. Here leats were built, and land drained over the centuries was used for industrial purposes. Most Exonians recognised Exe Island as the land from Head Weir to New Bridge Street. The land between the Higher and Lower Leats contained its own community, with the foundry of Parkins at its heart. An entrance was created to Exe Island when New Bridge Street was constructed; this went right under the road and into the heart of the area: a notice stated 'Exe Island Entrance'. From the mid-1960s Exe Island was radically changed, as the construction of Western Way swept away much of its character.

In October 1960 Exeter was to experience some of the worst flooding in its history. Millions of gallons of water were to overflow from the River Exe into St Thomas and other low-lying areas. The devastation was to affect over 1,000 properties in the city. Flooding was not new to Exeter, however, as it had a history of such problems. The result of this was the instigation of a major flood relief scheme. Its construction completely changed the look of the river Exe as it flows past the city: it is now incarcerated behind concrete defences. This photograph shows Okehampton Street totally unpassable.

The House That Moved, 1961. In the postwar period one of Exeter's oldest buildings was to gain world-wide publicity. No. 16 Edmund Street stood on the corner of Frog Street and Edmund Street, and has been dated to around 1430. By the 1930s the building was in poor condition. The ground floor was originally a shop, with accommodation above. With the planned creation of Western Way, the building was directly in the way. As it was of great antiquity a preservation order stopped it from being removed. In 1961 the building was lifted off its site and winched up to a new site at the corner of West Street. It has ever since been known as 'The House That Moved'.

The early fifteenth century property is shown fully restored and awaiting a new occupier, *c.* 1962.

Henry Wykes arrived in Exeter in 1914 and took over 1 Exe Bridge, a daylight studio. Because of his success in taking portraits of soldiers who were home from the First World War he moved premises to the prestigious Bedford Circus. Blitzed out in 1942, he moved to Northernhay Place. Henry Wykes was a prolific photographer, and the Wykes Studio created an archive of 42,000 images of the city. Without the work of Henry and his partner Marjorie Hockmuth the visual record of Exeter's history this century would be so much poorer. The studio closed in 1974, and all its photographs were retained for posterity by the author.

St Mary Major's Church, Cathedral Yard, 1965. In this century many people have not been able to understand why another church dominated the entrance to the Cathedral. Built in 1865, St Mary Major's Church replaced an earlier Norman church. This second church (shown) fell into disuse and was taken down in 1970. Archaeological excavations uncovered a Saxon Minster below the church foundations which pre-dated the Cathedral. More importantly, the most extensive Roman military barracks and bath house in the country were uncovered. The site had therefore been the earliest religious site in the city and had pre-dated the site of today's Cathedral.

Head Weir Mill, 1966. This substantial paper mill at the bottom of Exe Street has now been extensively remodelled and changed into a pub. In the eighteenth century fulling mills were advertised for sale on the site. Two years later a new paper mill was built to manufacture 'all types of paper'. At Head Weir water is diverted from the river Exe into the Higher and Lower Leats, which in the past operated the city's mills.

Interior view of Head Weir Paper Mill with paper bales.

Exeter Gasworks, seen here in about 1970, has for a very long time been a feature of the city's riverside. Its huge gasometers are a landmark today, even though the gasworks was much reduced with the introduction of natural gas. The works was created in 1836 and became the most important industry in the area. After closure in 1973 most of the buildings were demolished. Large quantities of coal, the fuel source, were stored at the edge of the canal. The Welcome Inn on the canal side was the last pub in the area to use gas lighting.

Mansfield's, 38 North Street. This building was one of Exeter's major losses this century – a merchant's house dating back to approximately 1500, and rebuilt in the seventeenth century. The building was demolished in 1972 as part of the Guildhall Shopping Centre development. Today its site, on the eastern side of the street, is the unsightly side of the shopping centre: the whole character of the street was eliminated here. The façade of the building was typical of other seventeenth-century buildings in Exeter and should have been retained.

The gallery of 38 North Street before demolition, 1972. Originally 38 North Street had an open hall with an arched braced roof, with the main walls built in Heavitree stone. Numerous original fifteenth-century features were found: fireplaces, early windows, hearths and ovens all came to light. A seventeenth-century ceiling was also discovered. One feature uncovered was the original gallery in the inner court, shown in this photograph, which was taken by the late Jacqueline Warren, an Exeter freelance writer and local historian.

The old Wool Hall, Goldsmith Street, 1979. Today, when people enter Marks & Spencer by its Goldsmith Street entrance, they may not realise that the arched structure under which they walk is a copy of the façade of a building which stood on the site previously. The building was the Wool Hall belonging to Lear, Brown and Dunsford, the woollen merchants. The decorative stone frontage hid a fascinating early Victorian interior which was completely panelled in pine planking with large wide shelves to carry bolts of cloth. Substantial wooden counters, staircase and balcony added to the attraction. Original gas lighting was still in situ. The new Marks & Spencer development was to destroy this building, but an architectural copy of the façade was integrated into the design for the rear entrance. Other features from similar buildings were also introduced.

The postwar redevelopment of High Street, seen here in 1979, was to create a thoroughfare almost 50 per cent wider than previously. The continued flow of two-way traffic was to be a problem as the number of vehicles increased in the '70s and '80s. A new word was being used – pedestrianisation. The city has not as yet committed itself to a totally traffic-free shopping environment. The postwar redevelopment did not cater for residents in the central area, and the social life of Exeter suffered as a result. Over the last fifteen years it has been recognised that there were flaws in the old scheme: major efforts have been made to soften the early architecture and to introduce gardens, public art and street furniture. Now there is major controversy about a plan to redevelop totally the area of Princesshay and Bedford Street. It is hoped that much will be learnt from what has passed.

1980–2000

Exeter University, August 1999. The ancient deer park on the edge of Exeter known in early times as the Manor of Duryard is today the site of Exeter University. The grounds of the university were once part of the Streatham Estate and they are still renowned for the collection of mature trees and plants from all over the world. Thousands of students come to one of the finest universities in England every year to study the arts, education, engineering, law, science, social studies and other aspects of academic life. Exeter University is a world leader in some fields of study and innovation, and is a major employer in the city.

Above: High Street, 1980. What was once an interesting group of buildings is now largely rebuilt. All the structures are supported by upright columns creating a covered walkway. The central building is new and was once the premises of Timothy White's, the chemist. The two bay windows shown are originals but from another building. The façade was created to give the impression of age.

The old and the new High Street, 1980. The building of C & A in High Street was to be one of the most controversial developments to happen in Exeter for many years. A fine façade had extended down Queen Street and around the corner into High Street. All was demolished and C & A built. Its next-door neighbour was a fine sixteenth-century house, from which the whole interior was removed, only its façade being left standing. The structure is supported by steel columns at its base and the façade plays no part in the building created behind it. The windows are curtained.

The new entrance to Gandy Street from High Street, 1980.

Exeter High Street, *c.* 1980. With the setting back of the High Street, the whole side of 229 High Street was exposed. Today this has been used for an attractive wall mural. The dominating Lloyds Bank and adjacent buildings were to take the place of some of Exeter's most well-known shops and businesses, including the Commercial Union, Bruford's, Ford Signs, Wippel Bros and the Devon & Somerset Stores. All had been blitzed.

Exeter High Street from St Stephen's Church, August 1999. The High Street is today divided between old and new. The division clearly marks the area devastated by the blitz of 1942 and the remaining original street. Beyond Dingles a wealth of differing architecture intrigues the visitor with a variety of styles, colour and shape. The properties are on a more human scale, and in this centre section we have some of the city's oldest properties. On the right is seen the wall mural of 229 High Street.

High Street, August 1999. The High Street is shown with mature trees, seating and other public facilities. The street is now a candidate for total pedestrianisation, because of the overwhelming number of buses.

Princesshay, August 1999. On 21 October 1949 HRH Princess Elizabeth opened the new Princesshay. At the time there was just a commemorative feature, and in front of her was waste ground. It was to become one of the first pedestrian precincts in the country. The vision for Princesshay can be claimed by Thomas Sharpe, a planner employed to make recommendations for the rebuilding of Exeter. His vision was that Princesshay should feature a major view of the Cathedral. This was acted upon, and today the lamp posts in Princesshay line up with the corner of the north tower of the Cathedral. Princesshay has been livened up with flower beds and, only in recent years, tables and chairs.

Cathedral Close, August 1999. Every year over 400,000 people come to Exeter Cathedral to view its splendours. Their visits boost the local economy and are a vital asset to the city. Exeter, as the administrative capital of the county, needs further recognition as a tourism destination and in recent years far more effort has been placed on marketing the city. Today, however, Exeter lacks further attractions to keep people in the city, and with the removal of much of its heritage over the last century, valuable assets have been lost. Far greater investment is needed in tourism as the city approaches the new millennium to ensure a more vibrant future.

View of the Quay from the City Wall, August 1999. Over the last fifteen years a great deal of work has been put into breathing life back into the Quayside area. A new footbridge over the River Exe created a circular route around the riverside. The riverside development of Haven Banks into apartments was to lose a further opportunity for creating leisure facilities. The city is still struggling to create an area of interest for visitors.

Western Way, August 1999. The decision to create an inner bypass to the south of Exeter was to result in an enormous amount of demolition and radical changes to parts of the city's townscape. It was to have a profound effect as it swept away many areas which were familiar to residents. The creation of Western Way at the junction with South Street was to lead to the City Wall being partially destroyed. All from the wall down to the riverside was bulldozed to create the new road. A new footbridge was placed over the road giving better access to the Quay. A Roman-style tower leads down to the new Coombe Street car park.

Broadwalk House, August 1999. From 1952 an extensive car park was created on the blitzed site at the top of Southernhay. Over twenty years later the car park was removed and the site was used for the construction of a building which was out of scale in an area famed for its fine Regency terraces. Although plans had been put forward to recreate the original style of the terraces these were not accepted, and the present huge red brick building was constructed.

Exeter Quay looking to the Basin, August 1999. With the 1960s floods a huge scheme was put under way to protect Exeter from flooding. The river banks were stockpiled and are now steel sided. The scheme has proved effective with a large concrete overflow at Kings Arms Sluice. The basin (centre) and its warehouses are at present receiving little use. Most of the area around the basin, which was industrial, has now been used for housing. At present the electricity generating station is being viewed for development.

Exeter Quayside, August 1999. At the turn of the century Exeter Quayside was in a steep decline and by the 1970s was no longer of interest as a commercial port. A major initiative by the City Council was responsible for the restoration of a number of buildings over a fifteen-year period.

Kings Wharf Warehouses, August 1999. This commodious warehouse built in 1835 now has a new lease of life. Originally for the storage of goods from seagoing ships, both warehouses have been converted to offices. The interiors of both buildings were completely removed. While a substantial pub operates from the building shown and there are other businesses in the cellars, the offices above have done little to improve the amount of activity in the area.

Haven Banks, August 1999. Haven Banks housing and the new Cricklepit footbridge create a new riverside view for Exeter. A ferry has operated from this site since 1641. The vessel today is still operated manually with a wire stretched across the river.

The Quay, August 1999. Visitors to the Quay have opportunities to explore part of the river and the Exeter Ship Canal by boat. Constructed in the mid-1600s the Exeter Ship Canal is the oldest pound lock canal in England and could be a much greater asset. There is no better way to come to Exeter than by the Ship Canal: superb views are obtained of the Exe Estuary, Topsham, Exminster Marshes and of the city overlooking the River Exe.

The Exeter Ship Canal is one of the most important stretches of fresh water in the county. It is no longer used by commercial shipping and its role has changed to one of leisure. Half of the canal stretches through a major conservation area, and it is one of the best places for birdwatching in the county. In the past it has been suggested that the canal should be filled in and turned into a road. Happily these days we have a more enlightened outlook.

Acknowledgements

The author would like to thank the citizens of Exeter for their interest and support over the last 25 years in preserving the visual history of Exeter.